when the daffodils die

by
Darah Schillinger

Thank you :)

Darah Schillinger

YELLOW ARROW
PUBLISHING

Baltimore, Maryland, USA

when the daffodils die
Copyright © 2022 by Yellow Arrow Publishing
All rights reserved.

Library of Congress Control Number: 2022940596
ISBN (paperback): 979-8-9850704-2-2

Cover art and interior images by Alexa Laharty (Instagram @alexaelisabeth). Interior design by Yellow Arrow Publishing. For more information, see yellowarrowpublishing.com.

when the daffodils die is dedicated to my parents for supporting me always, to my partner for loving me despite distance, to everyone who read and reread to reassure me, and to the Mother that made us all.
I love you.

"someone told me once that their bones are like trees and I laughed" was published by St. Mary's College of Maryland's literary magazine, *AVATAR*, in December 2021

Contents

dedication & acknowledgment	i
ripe	3
distance	5
someone told me once that their bones are like trees and I laughed	7
winter in Pennsylvania	9
couples therapy.	11
cloudy days	13
herbal medicine	15
Eden	17
blackberries	19
driver's ed	21
The Romantics (1798–1837)	23
Brood X	25
November 25, 2020, 5:14 pm	27
multiverse	29
untitled	31
thinning	35
I love meeting people lined with tattoos	37
lover(s)	39

Why Mars and Venus Collide	41
Mother's Day	43
I eat cherries like apples	45
Michigan: The Milk Carton Kids	47
marriage	49
untitled	51
sublime	53
overripe	55
I think it means something to be young	57
dreams	59
untitled	61
Before the Earth Swallows the Sky	63
the daffodils die	65
the women of "Why Mars and Venus Collide"	67
About the Author	71

WHEN THE DAFFODILS DIE

ripe

I am unfurled
open and wide
hands shoved deep—
the deepest chasms between my collarbone
into the space between my ribs
where white daisies grow
and yellow roses prick my lungs
where fields of grass and budded fruit blossom and drop
into the layers of my flesh
where the sun pulses
gently and my heart,
ripe for picking,
falls full onto the earth.

distance

I want his smell sunk into my skin
at the temples
where the hair meets my face.
I want to smell him in my pillow
late at night and early
in the mornings after he's gone
and left me with nothing but my thoughts and my saturated hairline.

what can I do when he leaves but wait for him to come back
just as it all starts to fade from my sheets
when nothing but my fingers have touched my lips in days,
the taste of almonds is gone from my tongue,
and I've finally washed the brown rings he's left in my mugs
what can I do?
nothing
but wait for the smell to fade just in time
for his shoes to return to my door,
laced and waiting for him
as I do.

someone told me once that their bones are like trees and I laughed

it was meant as a joke, but not the kind you laugh at
the kind in passing that are heavy because they're a little true
and I laughed anyway because I liked the picture it made
in the kitchen sun
my bones suddenly heavy
as if they could grow leaves, too

winter in Pennsylvania

the fields turned a mid December brown as the sky turned gray
the branches stripped bare of leaves
the grass shivering under frost,
the ground nothing more than frozen mud where
lines of broken plants stuck up sharp from the beige soil.
my body hairs resemble that brown of December now,
shooting out of cold pinkish flesh in the country wind
like the plants I push past and I wonder
what would happen if I kept the windows down as I drove,
the gray air woven in my hair, the smell of a Pennsylvania winter
clinging heavy in my pores, though I'm just passing through?
it would consume me, I think,
wear me down into the white roads
stamp me into the cold country soil
until I am finally
dust
and air.

couples therapy.

pull on the blades of grass caught
between your ring finger and thumb
take a sip of berry wine
drink in the night the way she drinks in the image of you
right beside her, damp from dew and
shivering like the grass you pluck.
you won't kiss her but you both want to—and oh how it must feel
to be the moon
watching what might have been,
heavy and bright,
as you unfold into   nothing.

cloudy days

on cloudy days i'd lay at the very edge of the bed on my back
in the cushy spot next to the window to keep the center from dipping
the spot right beneath the water stain on the ceiling.
sometimes i'd stay on the mattress
hands dirty gray from graphite
bare feet propped on the pillow,
head on the sheets or under the curtains,
and wait to see if i could feel the world stop turning
if i held my breath.
it was a good use of the day when the sky was full
to watch the trees sway
and think about abortion rights
or privilege
or poverty.

sometimes on those cloudy days dads would mow their lawns,
and i daydreamed of the sky opening up
and their shouts as they abandon their weed wackers in the yard
wet and angry at the sky
ungrateful that the world gives them water
to grow the grass they love to cut.

herbal medicine

Pour dried lavender buds and reassurance into the clogged wounds
of your chest and		breathe in
wait, wait until the heavy fog recedes.

Do you see the sky? Have the clouds lifted from the pavement?
There's a fever in your cheeks.
Here, let drops of peppermint oil and patience drip-drip
from your palms like
VapoRub for the rattled soul,

cough out the wetness from your lungs
and the weight from your mind,
let your blood boil over and heal the heavy sick
the doctors cannot see and the
patient cannot point to.

Oh honey, you're suffering.

Eden

Lilith, do you miss the garden?
the fruit trees and figs,
the smooth stones and sun?
do you miss the paradise
stripped clean from your flesh
and the husband you could not love
before love and time existed?

You, cast from the garden,
replaced by another
cracked directly from the rib—
the rib made only to eat the very fruit god supplied her
so he could call it sin and take paradise
away.

Lilith, do you think of Eve, when you run with your night creatures?
when you fly into the dark air, hated but free?
are you grateful you ran from paradise
before the weight of biblical sin
fell forever on your feminine shoulders,
rather a demon than a woman to blame?

You, Lilith, are proof we were never made to obey.

blackberries

look like nighttime and taste like the very end of summer,
sweet like late August just before September sweaters set in.
they stain your lips and
you open your mouth wide to show me when they get caught
in your back molars because you
know I hate how dark they are against the off white of your teeth—
your lips are purple again, purple and not black and I haven't
stopped wondering
if I kiss you once and never again
will it feel like dying?
because I haven't even tried, and my lungs feel like the seeds
between your teeth
crushed and stuck in the cavities of my chest.

driver's ed

my mother has a habit of distracting herself

it happens mostly in the car,
on highways and long stretches of white road bleached from the sun,
when she'll stop mid conversation
to point out a hawk perched on the nearest light pole
or the tan blur of deer fur in the brush along 95
and she'll say,

"look baby"

and I rarely see what she's pointing at,
frustrated that she's now forgotten the sentence she cut off.

my mother has a habit of distracting herself with the dead animals
along the shoulder,
always whispering,

"poor thing"

in the air between her mouth and the steering wheel,
nose wrinkled in grief,
and I always search for the pile of wretched flesh she's found
in varying states of decomposition.

when I began driving, I told myself I wouldn't get distracted
as she does.
my instructor said it was dangerous, and I always pictured
the disapproving look she would give
my mother if she watched her drive along 95.

But even now I find myself alone in the car, eyes on the white roads,

driving past flattened
squirrels opossums birds deer

and mouthing

poor thing

to my own steering wheel.

The Romantics (1798–1837)

it's poetry
finding friendship before they've made love to you
before they've tasted the skin over your spine, in
cars and
closets and
twin beds
before they've pressed their palms to yours and breathed
damp breath in the shell of your ear,
knowing their cheeks are red even though you can't see them.
when you've found the person who kisses you five different ways,
the person to spend yellow summer days with
alongside those navy nights,
the person with a cup of tea and a smile after one of your hard ones.
it's canvas to say,
"I love you and that is the beginning and end of everything,"
but it's art when you mean it
even after the candles are blown out and the lovemaking is done.

Brood X

my dear cicadas
what is your purpose? to eat?
my peaches are dead

crunchy insect shells
litter the ground, fat bodies
bounce off the windshield

from ground to treetop seventeen years, a long time
just to scream, fuck, die

(i love you. . . ?)

November 25, 2020, 5:14 pm

I find myself on the rotting wood steps of our back porch
under the almost-winter skies of mid November
cool on my hot flesh and bare toes
the scent of apple skins and cinnamon in my hair.
We have a peach tree
tucked away and crooked on the side of our hill,
lopsided with age and withered fruit.
A few green leaves cling to the tips of its branches
and I watch them flutter,
the brown arms silhouetted against the ever-darkening sky.
I find myself leaving the steps,
wondering at the hardened pits littering its branches
from years of rot,
and a rabbit scurries under the fence at the sound of me.
I grab a pit, cold and solid in my fist, and watch it fall to the ground
between my feet
a dull thud against the earth,
lost amongst the dried leaves and
too far gone to grow.

multiverse

what if we all have lived before
and we simply forget what living was like

fresh and empty and screaming our infant throats raw,
pink and shivering under fluorescent lights
exiting our last life through the warmth of the womb

(reincarnation takes time)

white skies in summer seem emptier than nothing at all / than blue light scattered across the vast open air / than dirt. / I told her that and she laughed, / she laughed like rain in the early morning, / when the night was still bright and the day was still asleep, and I kissed her. / I almost stopped, because she was no longer laughing, and that laugh was everything, and I would have almost rather listened than tasted her. / (almost, almost sounds like a nonword when you say it enough, but my tongue feels heavy from the thought of it now.) / I think I loved her / can I say love if I don't know? / she was something deeper than me, like paint peeling off a cracked wall only to reveal the vibrant wallpaper beneath it, / too loud for the former inhabitants / and I loved that. / I loved her. / I can still picture how I peeled back with my hands / can still see her smiling, / skin like oranges and just as fragrant. / she urged me with her summer eyes, and I was so so careful not to puncture her soft flesh, / running citrus down her dress. / I was careful with her because   she made me more than a white sky in June / more than blue light air / more than dirt / and it still means something /

// even now, I am more//

thinning

the crape myrtles
rub their long fingers together
rattling like drying, brittle bones
and I listen to you laugh under them
competing with them
like your joy could overtake theirs
twisting together into a cacophony of something
I've never heard before
and may never hear again

I love meeting people lined with tattoos

coffee cup people

their own names written on them in sharpie
cardboard skin

the paper people

the people who come from trees
deep punctured
dark-marked flesh
the ones with honeycomb thighs
sprawling ink tumbleweeds caught in cactuses

the people who mortalize art
it dies with them
ink turned to ash with their bones
on display only as long as the canvas

lover(s)

I cut up peaches in a white ceramic bowl
and they sat there on the windowsill
drying from the summer heat but
still orange
my fingers a little red from
where there used to be a pit
staining the front of my dress
—a color red that lingers the way they do

Why Mars and Venus Collide

John Gray claims that the left inferior parietal lobe is more developed in men whereas the right is more developed in women:

". . . the left side of the brain has more to do with more linear, reasonable, and rational thought, while the right side of the brain is more emotional, feeling, and intuitive."

of course

of course we are irrational emotional nonlinear

it's natural

it's in the brain

women can't think logically

(Mary Jackson, Susan La Flesche, Cordelia Fine, Tu Youyou)*

That is, until a man argued we could:

"Our most accurate anatomical investigations do not uncover any difference between men and women in this part of the body [the head]. The brain of women is exactly like ours."
-Poullain

But at least we still can't compete with men physically

(Jackie Tonawanda, Billie Jean King, Eri Yoshida)

Too delicate

(Jackie Mitchell)

Too slow

(Allyson Felix, Alysia Montaño)

Must be born a man to be such an outlier

(Serena Williams, Caster Semenya)

or maybe this was never about the "natural limitations" of the cisgender woman—maybe you believe in yourselves so much and you believe in us so little
that you cannot fathom the power a real woman has when she is finally given the opportunity

(stop blaming nature for your prejudice)

*interested in learning more about the amazing women mentioned here? you'll find short bios for each toward the end of *when the daffodils die*

Mother's Day

our Mother's love is constant and vibrant and holds me
fast to her chest
when romance leaves deep bloody crescents in the skin of my arms
and a throbbing hollow dissatisfaction
in the clay of my stomach

Mother loves me even when I don't love her back.

(Blessed be.)

I eat cherries like apples

and you pop the whole fruit in your mouth
carving out the seed with your tongue
but the pits
stained both our lips the same red
dripping the same juice down our fingers
to match the blood
in our cheeks

Michigan: The Milk Carton Kids

gray clouds,
turned tawny in the fading light,
float overhead, heavy with water
overtaking the summer sky and
rain dampened sunset.
beams gathered in patches of yellow cloth, yellow field,
double yellow lines
endlessly stretching
the air wet and hot, anticipating, waiting,
hot against my face, wet in my lungs.

the clouds' silent thunder
matches mine

marriage

I fall in love daily
with the sky and the sea and
the pollen watering my eyes
in winter storms and the heavy sound of
rainwater falling
            falling
                      and I fall
again and again
with or without you

tell me what we are kept here
for if not to cry through the
night
and sleep
in the arms of a lover   ?

sublime

I keep my eyes trained to the ground
in case I crush something smaller beneath my bare feet

like the pliant bodies of half-dried earthworms,
soft but solid under my fingers
or the brown grasshoppers scattering from the dusty brick
back into the underbrush

but I really want to stare into the sky
between the green leaf clouds above me
into the belly of the atmosphere
and ask the birds

who gave god that color blue?

overripe

you cracked me open violently
with feather light touches
with sweet words that hushed my worries and gentle hands—
soft hands that lifted me
from the rotting oak I hollowed out and buried my bones in—
hands that cradled my brittle body
naked and overripe on the forest floor.
my bark chips lay overgrown
from people who never held me
from being too much for those
who remain too little
from pasts you help me replace with memories of us
our branches heavy now
with budding fruit.

I think it means something to be young

to have your head full of old music and new poetry

driving with both arms
ready and aimed at the sky
like birds
to be so full of loose paper
you become flammable
without even knowing it's there

maybe I'm wrong
maybe I just want to mean something when it's cloudy at bedtime
maybe I'm just tired again

maybe I'll like me more in the morning

dreams

I hope I never learn to remove you from my bones
my skin smelling of yours
my legs soft from your lips
the clothes I take from you
still laundry fresh and sweet
your scent mingled and finally overtaken by my own
with each passing day.
I hope you think of me like this
when you lay under windows and the night air seeps in
closing the gaping weeks with unwashed
pillowcases and
loose coconut ChapStick
like I do.
I hope you stay up dreaming about how the moon might look
with me under it   dreaming of when
I'll fill a space in our bed and
you can reach out
just to feel the bare flesh of my shoulder
knowing **I am real.**

how foolish we can be to believe all love comes without loss
that love defies impermanence and lasts until we are full
and brimming with mutual readiness for the end.
love can conquer distance and time and uncertainty
and it can
break
fall apart
die,
still meaning something after

"there's peace in acknowledging the death of things"

based on a Tweet by @thekayanova

Before the Earth Swallows the Sky

I want to feel hot June on my skin and
let my shaky hands carry empty fistfuls of sand from the shore
until my footpads are soggy white and every last grain
slips through my wrinkled fingers.
I want to fly on rusty swing sets
so high my joints hit the clouds and my blood rushes
to the very top of my head.
I want to run a bath so hot
the spotted skin of my chest turns pink and swollen
soaked in lavender syrup and soft petals I took from the stems.
I want to kiss a stranger
maybe even on the lips—just once
under a tree or by a soft windowsill in spring.
I want to hold a hand in mine and aim my ragged laughter at the sky
as night falls blue on the ceiling
and it breathes nice and low.
I want to watch my hot breath blow
into the morning on the coldest day in January
my fingers—now purple—held gently by someone who loves me.
I want to sing a lullaby to a child with my own eyes
much younger and softer than my own
watch as they close and drift away into dreams.
I want to feel love and give love one last time
before the box closes and the birds fly away
before the Earth swallows the sky and
time rocks me once again
to sleep.

the daffodils die

and have crumpled brown into the soil
before May even comes,
leaving the gulch empty and green
laid bare before the brackish water.
heralding spring with the rot.

what a devastating way to fall in love.

a very brief look at the amazing, incredible women of "Why Mars and Venus Collide"

Allyson Felix (b. 1985) – American track and field athlete who is a 2012 Olympic champion, a three-time world champion (2005–2009), a two-time Olympic silver medalist (2004 and 2008), and the 2011 world bronze medalist in the 200 m sprint. Allyson, along with Alysia Montaño and Kara Goucher, is credited with stirring public outcry over Nike's refusal to guarantee salary protections for its pregnant athletes, prompting the sportswear brand to subsequently expand its maternity policy in 2019. Find out more at allysonfelix.com.

Cordelia Fine (b. 1975) – Canadian-born British philosopher of science, psychologist, and writer. She is a full professor of history and philosophy at the University of Melbourne, Australia. Cordelia has written numerous books, including *Testosterone Rex*, which won the Royal Society Book Price in 2017. She is noted for coining the term 'neurosexism'. Find out more at cordelia-fine.com.

Virne Beatrice "Jackie" Mitchell Gilbert (b. 1913, d. 1987) – American baseball player and first female pitcher in professional baseball history. She was only 17 years old when she pitched for the Chattanooga Lookouts Class AA minor league baseball team and struck out Babe Ruth and Lou Gehrig. Soon after, she retired and Major League Baseball would eventually ban the signing of women to contracts in 1952 until it was finally lifted in 1992.

Mary Jackson (b. 1921, d. 2005) – American mathematician and aerospace engineer at the National Advisory Committee for Aeronautics (NACA), which was succeeded by the National Aeronautics and Space Administration (NASA) in 1958. That same year, she became NASA's first black female engineer. In her role as manager of both the Federal Women's Program and the Affirmative Action Program, Mary was influential in the hiring and promotion of women in NASA's science, engineering, and mathematics careers.

Billie Jean King (b. 1943) – American former world No. 1 tennis player. She won over 39 major titles and was U.S. captain of the Federation Cup. Billie Jean is an advocate for gender equality and a pioneer for equality and social justice. She founded the Women's Tennis Association and the Women's Sports Foundation. Find out more at billiejeanking.com.

Alysia Montaño (b. 1986) – American middle distance runner and a six-time U.S. Outdoor Track and Field Championships 800 m winner. She gained publicity in 2014 for competing while eight months pregnant and in 2017 while five months pregnant. Along with Allyson Felix and Kara Goucher, Alysia advocated that pregnancy does not equal the end of a woman's athletic career.

Susan La Flesche Picotte (b. 1865, d. 1915) – Native American doctor and reformer of the late 19th century. She is acknowledged as one of the first Indigenous peoples, and the first Indigenous woman, to earn a medical degree. Susan was an active social reformer and physician and worked to help other Omaha tribal members navigate the Office of Indian Affairs.

Mokgadi Caster Semenya OIB (b. 1991) – South African middle-distance runner and winner of two Olympic gold medals and three World Championships in the women's 800 m. Caster is an intersex woman forced to undergo tests and take medication to compete and eventually banned from events by the World Athletics. She filed an appeal with the European Court of Human Rights against the restrictions. OIB, or the Order of Ikhamanga, is a South African national honor.

Jackie Tonawanda (b. 1933, d. 2009) – American female heavyweight boxer in the 1970s and 1980s. In 1975, she sued the New York State Athletic Commission for denying her a professional boxing license because of her gender. The case was decided in her favor though it did not overturn the law in New York against women boxing. The law was eventually overturned in 1977 after a second case brought by Cathy Davis. Jackie is the first woman to box in Madison Square Garden.

Serena Williams (b. 1981) – American professional tennis player ranked singles world No. 1 by the Women's Tennis Association for 319 weeks. She has won 23 Grand Slam singles titles and 14 major women's doubles titles with her sister, Venus. Serena has also won four Olympic gold medals, including three in women's doubles with her sister. She is the highest-earning woman athlete of all time. Find out more at serenawilliams.com.

Eri Yoshida (吉田 えり) (b. 1992) – Japanese professional baseball player known for her sidearm knuckleball pitch. In 2008, when she was 16 years old, she became the first woman drafted by a Japanese men's professional baseball team.

Tu Youyou (屠呦呦) (b. 1930) – Chinese pharmaceutical chemist and malariologist. She discovered artemisinin and dihydroartemisinin, used to treat malaria. Tu received the 2011 Lasker Award in clinical medicine and the 2015 Nobel Price in Physiology or Medicine as the first Chinese Nobel laureate.

how many more amazing women can you think of?

DARAH SCHILLINGER graduated from St. Mary's College of Maryland in May 2022, studying english literature with a double minor in creative writing and philosophy. She previously interned for the literary magazine *EcoTheo Review* in summer 2020 and has had poetry published in her school literary journal, *AVATAR*, in the Spillwords Press Haunted Holidays series for 2020, and in *Yellow Arrow Journal* **UpSpring** (Vol. VII, No. 1). Darah currently lives in Perry Hall, Maryland, with her parents, and in her free time, she likes to write poetry and paint. She plans to pursue an MS in professional writing and hopes to establish a career in publishing after its completion.

Thank you for supporting independent publishing.

Yellow Arrow Publishing is a nonprofit supporting writers that identify as women. Visit YellowArrowPublishing.com for information on our publications, workshops, and writing opportunities.

CPSIA information can be obtained
at www.ICGtesting.com
Printed in the USA
JSHW041448090722
27834JS00001B/16